The Road

to

Hundred Million Dollars

Mastering the 9-figure mindset.

Roy S. Ferranti

THE ROAD

to

$100 MILLION

Mastering the 9-figure mindset.

Roy S. Ferranti

Introduction

The Nine-Figure Mindset

In the ever-evolving landscape of wealth creation, there exists a realm reserved for those with audacious dreams and an unshakeable belief in their ability to achieve them. This book is your guide to that realm, where the boundaries of financial potential are pushed far beyond the ordinary, where fortunes climb into nine figures, and where the mindset to reach such heights is forged.

We often marvel at individuals who have amassed vast wealth, attributing their success to luck, opportunity, or a special set of circumstances. While these factors may play a role, the true secret lies in the mindset. It's a mindset that is not exclusive to a chosen few; it's one that can be cultivated, learned, and mastered by anyone willing to embark on this journey.

"the road to $100 Million: Mastering the Nine-Figure Mindset" is a roadmap to transform your thinking, your financial prospects, and ultimately, your life. It's a blueprint for reaching that elusive nine-figure milestone, not merely as a distant dream but as a tangible destination.

This book is not a promise of overnight riches or a guarantee of effortless success. Instead, it's an invitation to embark on a transformational journey. You'll explore the psychology of wealth, learn to break free from the shackles of limiting beliefs, and harness the power of visualisation to set audacious financial goals.

We'll delve into diverse strategies for wealth building, from astute investments to entrepreneurial ventures and the magic of passive income. Real-life success stories will inspire you, while insights into risk management, networking, and the art of giving back will shape your journey.

Challenges will arise; setbacks will test your resolve. But armed with the nine-figure mindset, you'll learn to adapt, grow, and thrive even in the face of adversity. This is not just about accumulating wealth; it's about creating a lasting legacy and a life of purpose.

As you turn the pages of this book, you'll find actionable advice, exercises, and resources to guide you on your quest. You'll gain not only the knowledge but the confidence to stride confidently on your unique path to financial mastery.

So, are you ready to embark on this extraordinary journey, to unlock the potential within you, and to step onto the road to $100 million? The adventure begins now. Welcome to the world of the Nine-Figure Mindset.

Part I

Mindset

In the world of wealth creation, where fortunes rise to unprecedented heights, the concept of mindset stands as the cornerstone upon which these towering edifices of affluence are built. Imagine your mindset as the inner compass that guides your financial journey, charting the course to your desired destination. In this exploration, we delve deeply into the profound implications of a mindset primed for nine-figure success.

At the heart of the matter lies the pivotal concept of limiting beliefs. These are the invisible chains that shackle the aspirations of many, whispering tales of inadequacy and unworthiness. Limiting beliefs often take root in early experiences or societal conditioning, echoing in our thoughts and decisions, and ultimately determining the bounds of our financial aspirations.

In this part of our journey, we confront these insidious adversaries head-on. We unearth the origins of these beliefs, bringing them to the light of awareness. Recognition is the first step, and it's followed closely by strategies to dismantle these limiting constructs. By systematically dislodging these obstructions, we open ourselves to the immense possibilities that await those who dare to dream without constraint.

With the fertile ground of an unburdened mind, we sow the seeds of the abundance mentality. This is the shift from viewing the world through a lens of scarcity to one of boundless abundance. The abundance mentality recognizes that there are ample resources, opportunities, and success stories to go around. It thrives on the belief that one person's achievement does not diminish the opportunities available to others but rather creates new pathways.

This part invites you to embrace this transformative shift. Through practical exercises and mindset-shifting practices, you'll cultivate a mindset that magnetizes prosperity and opportunities. It's a mindset that fosters creativity, encourages collaboration, and breeds optimism in the face of challenges. With the abundance mentality as your compass, you'll navigate the financial landscape with confidence and resilience.

Finally, in the realm of the nine-figure mindset, goal setting is the compass needle that keeps you on course. Dreams alone are not enough; they require precise articulation and a clear plan of action. The fourth chapter reveals the art and science of setting goals that are not only audacious but actionable.

By crafting goals that are Specific, Measurable, Achievable, Relevant, and Time-bound (SMART), you'll create a roadmap that leaves no room for ambiguity. Yet, we take it a step further, delving into the power of visualization. Through this technique, you'll learn to vividly envision your goals, tapping into the subconscious mind's incredible ability to drive you towards them. Visualization makes your aspirations tangible, and as your mindset aligns with these vivid mental images, your actions naturally follow suit.

ONE

Overcoming Limiting Beliefs

Limiting beliefs are the silent saboteurs that lurk within our minds, whispering insidious doubts about our capabilities and potential. They are the mental barriers that hinder us from reaching for the stars and achieving financial greatness. In this exploration, we delve into the profound importance of identifying and overcoming these limiting beliefs to unlock your full financial potential.

The Origins of Limiting Beliefs

Limiting beliefs often take root in our formative years. They may stem from childhood experiences, societal conditioning, or even past failures. These beliefs fester quietly in our subconscious, casting shadows on our dreams and ambitions. Common examples include beliefs that we're not smart enough, not talented enough, or not deserving of wealth.

Understanding the origins of these beliefs is crucial. By tracing them back to their source, we can shine a light on the hidden narratives that have been silently guiding our financial decisions for years. It's akin to exposing the roots of a troublesome weed; only by understanding where it comes from can we effectively remove it from our mental landscape.

The Impact of Limiting Beliefs

The insidious nature of limiting beliefs lies in their ability to shape our reality. When we believe we're not capable of achieving financial success, we inadvertently sabotage our efforts. We settle for less, avoid risks, and shy away from opportunities. These beliefs become self-fulfilling prophecies, as our actions align with our negative expectations.

Moreover, limiting beliefs lead to a scarcity mindset, where we perceive a world of limited resources and competition, making us reluctant to take calculated risks. This mindset can hinder our ability to seize opportunities and create the wealth we desire.

Strategies for Overcoming Limiting Beliefs

Overcoming limiting beliefs is an essential step on the road to financial success. It's about challenging these beliefs and replacing them with empowering thoughts. Here are strategies to help you break free from their grip:

1. *Awareness*: The first step is recognizing and acknowledging your limiting beliefs. Journaling or talking to a trusted friend or therapist can be helpful in bringing these beliefs to the surface.
2. *Questioning*: Challenge the validity of these beliefs. Ask yourself, "Is this belief based on facts or assumptions?" Often, you'll find that these beliefs lack a solid foundation.
3. *Reframing*: Replace limiting beliefs with affirmations or empowering statements. For instance, if you believe you're not good with money,

reframe it as "I am capable of learning and managing my finances."

4. *Visualisation*: Use the power of visualization to imagine yourself achieving your financial goals. Visualization can help reprogram your subconscious mind to align with your aspirations.

5. *Action*: Take small steps toward your financial goals, even if you feel doubt. As you accumulate evidence of your capabilities, your confidence will grow, eroding the power of limiting beliefs.

Abundance Mentality

The abundance mentality is a profound shift in perspective that transforms the way we perceive the world and our place in it. It's the belief that resources, opportunities, and success are not finite but boundless, awaiting those who embrace this perspective. This mindset is the key to unlocking financial prosperity.

In an abundance mentality, the world is viewed as a place of limitless possibilities. Instead of fearing competition and scarcity, individuals with this mindset welcome challenges and see them as opportunities for growth. They believe that their success doesn't diminish others but, in fact, creates more opportunities for everyone.

This mindset fosters a sense of gratitude for what one has and an unwavering belief in what can be achieved. It encourages innovation, collaboration, and a willingness to take calculated risks. People with an abundance mentality are more likely to invest, start businesses, and explore new avenues for wealth creation.

Embracing the abundance mentality doesn't mean ignoring real-world challenges or denying the existence of scarcity in some areas. It's about choosing to focus on solutions and possibilities rather than dwelling on limitations. By adopting this mindset, you will not only transform your relationship with money but also your entire approach to life, leading to financial prosperity and a sense of fulfillment that extends far beyond wealth.

Goal Setting

Goal setting is the compass that guides you on your journey to financial mastery and, ultimately, the achievement of a nine-figure mindset. Goals serve as the map, plotting the course, and providing direction. They are the foundation upon which your financial success is built, transforming your dreams into concrete objectives.

The Power of Setting Goals

Setting goals is not merely an exercise in wishful thinking; it's a strategic process that propels you toward your aspirations. Goals provide clarity, purpose, and motivation. They give you something specific to aim for, breaking down your grand vision into actionable steps. When you set clear and compelling financial goals, you increase your likelihood of success exponentially.

SMART Goals: A Blueprint for Success

To set effective financial goals, it's crucial to follow the SMART framework:

1. *Specific*: Your goals should be precise and well-defined. Vague aspirations like "get rich" lack clarity. Instead, specify what "rich" means to you, such as "accumulating $100 million in assets by age 50."
2. *Measurable*: Goals must be quantifiable. You need a way to track your progress. In our example, the $100 million figure provides a measurable target.
3. *Achievable*: While goals should stretch you beyond your comfort zone, they should also be realistic. Setting an unattainable goal can lead to frustration. Ensure your goals are

achievable within your current circumstances and capabilities.

4. *Relevant*: Goals should align with your values and long-term vision. They should be relevant to your life and aspirations. Ask yourself if the goal is genuinely important to you.

5. *Time-bound*: A goal without a deadline is merely a dream. Set a specific timeframe for achieving your goal. In our example, the deadline is "by age 50."

Visualisation: Seeing Your Goals

Visualization is a powerful tool in goal setting. It involves creating vivid mental images of your goals as if they've already been achieved. When you visualize success, you're training your subconscious mind to align your actions with your goals. This technique can increase motivation and resilience.

Breaking Down Goals into Action Steps

Once you've defined your SMART goals, it's essential to break them down into actionable steps. These are the smaller, manageable tasks that move you closer to your ultimate goal. Creating a timeline and a to-do list for each step ensures you stay on track and motivated.

The Role of Flexibility

While setting goals is crucial, it's equally vital to remain flexible. Life is unpredictable, and circumstances change. Being open to adjusting your goals and strategies can prevent frustration and allow you to adapt to new opportunities or challenges.

Celebrating Milestones

As you make progress toward your financial goals, celebrate your achievements along the way. Acknowledging milestones reinforces your commitment and keeps your motivation high.

Part II

Wealth Building

Wealth building is a multifaceted journey that involves the strategic accumulation and management of assets and resources. It's a journey that transforms financial dreams into tangible reality. In this exploration, we delve into the art and science of wealth building, unraveling the key principles and strategies that lead to financial prosperity.

The Foundations of Wealth Building

1. *Financial Literacy*: Building wealth begins with knowledge. Understanding financial concepts, from budgeting to investing, is

fundamental. Financial literacy empowers individuals to make informed decisions and optimise their financial resources.

2. **Budgeting and Savings:** Budgeting provides a roadmap for managing income and expenses. Saving a portion of your income is the first step toward building wealth. Creating an emergency fund and consistently saving are essential habits.

Investment Strategies

1. **Diversification**: Spreading investments across various asset classes (stocks, bonds, real estate, etc.) helps manage risk. Diversification minimizes the impact

of poor-performing assets on your overall portfolio.

2. *Compounding*: Compound interest is a powerful wealth-building tool. It allows your money to earn interest, and then that interest earns interest. Over time, this can lead to significant wealth growth.

3. *Long-Term Perspective:* Successful wealth builders maintain a long-term view. They understand that market fluctuations are part of the journey and don't let short-term volatility deter them from their goals.

4. *Asset Allocation:* Allocating assets based on your financial goals and risk tolerance is crucial. The mix of investments in your portfolio should align with your objectives, whether it's wealth preservation or growth.

Entrepreneurship and Income Streams

1. *Multiple Income Streams*: Wealth builders often create multiple income streams. This can include side businesses, rental income, dividends from investments, or royalties from intellectual property.
2. *Entrepreneurship*: Starting a business can be a powerful wealth-building strategy. Successful entrepreneurs can generate substantial wealth through the growth and sale of their enterprises.

Real Estate as a Wealth-Building Asset

1. *Real Estate Investment*: Real estate, whether residential or commercial, is

a popular avenue for wealth building. It offers rental income, potential for property appreciation, and tax benefits.

2. *Real Estate Investment Trusts (REITs):* REITs provide a way for individuals to invest in real estate without owning physical properties. They offer dividends and the potential for capital appreciation.

Passive Income Streams

1. *Dividend Stocks:* Investing in dividend-paying stocks can provide a steady stream of passive income. Dividends are typically paid by stable, mature companies.

2. *Peer-to-Peer Lending*: Online platforms enable individuals to lend money to others and earn interest in return.

Risk Management and Wealth Preservation

1. *Diversification*: Beyond investment diversification, consider diversifying income streams and assets to protect wealth.
2. *Insurance*: Adequate insurance coverage safeguards against unexpected financial setbacks.
3. *Estate Planning:* Planning for the transfer of wealth to future generations is crucial. It involves wills, trusts, and tax strategies.

4. *Continuous Learning:* Staying informed about financial markets, investment opportunities, and evolving strategies is vital for adapting to changing circumstances.

TWO

Investment Strategies

Investment strategies are the blueprint for growing wealth and achieving financial goals. They encompass a diverse range of approaches, from conservative income generation to aggressive capital appreciation. In this comprehensive exploration, we delve into the intricacies of investment strategies, offering insights into their types, key principles, and the factors to consider when crafting your investment portfolio.

Types of Investment Strategies

1. *Income Investing*: This strategy prioritizes generating regular income from investments. It often involves assets like bonds, dividend-paying stocks, and real estate investment trusts (REITs). Income investors seek stable cash flows and are generally more risk-averse.

2. *Value Investing:* Value investors search for undervalued assets with the potential for long-term growth. They seek to buy assets at a discount to their intrinsic value. This strategy, popularized by Warren Buffett, requires in-depth research and patience.

3. *Growth Investing:* Growth investors focus on companies with high growth potential. They're willing to invest in stocks with high valuations in

anticipation of future appreciation. Technology and innovative sectors often attract growth investors.

4. *Diversification and Asset Allocation*: Diversification involves spreading investments across various asset classes (stocks, bonds, real estate, etc.) to manage risk. Asset allocation refers to the mix of these assets in a portfolio. Both are critical strategies for balancing risk and return.

5. *Passive vs. Active Investing:* Passive investors typically use index funds or exchange-traded funds (ETFs) to mimic the performance of a broad market index. Active investors, on the other hand, actively manage their portfolios, seeking to outperform the market.

6. *Value Averaging:* This strategy involves regularly investing a fixed amount, adjusting based on portfolio performance. It encourages buying more when prices are low and less when prices are high, maintaining a consistent investment discipline.

Key Principles of Investment Strategies

1. *Risk Tolerance:* Assess your risk tolerance honestly. It determines your ability to withstand market volatility. More aggressive strategies may yield higher returns but carry higher risks.
2. *Diversification*: Spread your investments across different asset classes to reduce risk. Diversification can be achieved through mutual

funds, ETFs, or owning a mix of assets.

3. *Time Horizon*: Consider your investment horizon. Longer horizons allow for more aggressive strategies, as short-term fluctuations have less impact on long-term goals.

4. *Costs and Fees:* Minimise investment costs and fees, as they can erode returns over time. Low-cost index funds and ETFs are popular choices for cost-conscious investors.

5. *Research and Due Diligence*: Invest time in researching potential investments. Understand the companies or assets you invest in, their financial health, and their growth potential.

6. *Emotional Discipline:* Emotional reactions to market fluctuations can

lead to poor investment decisions. Maintain a disciplined approach and avoid impulsive reactions to short-term market movements.

Factors to Consider in Building a Portfolio

1. *Asset Allocation*: Determine the mix of asset classes in your portfolio based on your goals, risk tolerance, and time horizon.
2. *Rebalancing*: Periodically adjust your portfolio to maintain your desired asset allocation. This ensures that your risk profile remains aligned with your goals.
3. *Tax Efficiency:* Consider tax implications when crafting your

portfolio. Tax-efficient investing can significantly impact after-tax returns.

4. *Review and Monitoring*: Regularly review your investments to assess performance and ensure alignment with your goals. Adjust your strategy as necessary.

5. *Liquidity*: Evaluate the liquidity of your investments. Some assets may be less liquid and require a longer investment horizon.

6. *Exit Strategy:* Define your exit strategy. Determine when and how you'll sell investments to meet financial goals or rebalance your portfolio.

Entrepreneurship

Entrepreneurship is the dynamic force that drives innovation, fuels economic growth, and shapes the future of industries. It's the art of identifying opportunities, taking calculated risks, and bringing ideas to life. In this extensive exploration, we delve into the multifaceted world of entrepreneurship, examining its significance, key principles, challenges, and the transformative impact it has on individuals and society.

The Significance of Entrepreneurship

1. *Economic Engine*: Entrepreneurship plays a pivotal role in economic development. Startups and small businesses create jobs, stimulate economic activity, and contribute significantly to a country's GDP.

2. *Innovation and Progress*:
   Entrepreneurs are the architects of innovation. They challenge the status quo, introduce new technologies, and disrupt existing markets. Innovative solutions improve our quality of life and drive progress.

3. **Wealth Creation:** Successful entrepreneurs often amass substantial wealth, contributing to personal financial prosperity. This wealth can be reinvested in new ventures, philanthropy, or job creation.

Key Principles of Entrepreneurship

1. *Identifying Opportunities:*
   Entrepreneurship begins with

recognizing opportunities in the market or identifying unmet needs. Successful entrepreneurs are keen observers of trends and customer behavior.

2. *Risk-Taking*: Entrepreneurship involves calculated risk-taking. Entrepreneurs are willing to invest time, money, and effort in pursuing opportunities, even in the face of uncertainty.

3. *Innovation and Creativity*: Innovation is the lifeblood of entrepreneurship. Entrepreneurs create novel solutions, products, or services that distinguish them from competitors.

4. *Market Research:* Understanding the target market is essential. Market research helps entrepreneurs tailor

their offerings to meet customer needs and preferences.

5. *Business Planning*: A solid business plan outlines the company's vision, mission, goals, and strategies. It serves as a roadmap for the business's growth.

6. *Resource Management:* Efficient allocation of resources, including capital, talent, and time, is crucial. Entrepreneurs often wear multiple hats and must prioritise tasks effectively.

7. *Adaptability*: Markets evolve, and entrepreneurs must adapt. Being open to change and responsive to market feedback is key to long-term success.

Types of Entrepreneurship

1. *Small Business Entrepreneurship:* These entrepreneurs typically operate local businesses, such as restaurants, retail stores, or service providers. They focus on serving local communities.

2. *Social Entrepreneurship:* Social entrepreneurs combine business principles with a commitment to addressing social or environmental issues. Their goal is to create positive societal impact alongside financial sustainability.

3. *Innovative or High-Tech Entrepreneurship:* Founders in this category create startups with innovative technology or solutions. They often seek venture capital funding for rapid growth.

4. *Serial Entrepreneurship:* Serial entrepreneurs start and manage multiple businesses over their careers. They thrive on the challenge of launching new ventures.

Challenges in Entrepreneurship

1. *Financial Risks:* Entrepreneurship involves financial risks. Many startups face capital constraints, and founders may invest their savings or seek external funding.
2. *Uncertainty*: Market dynamics can be unpredictable. Entrepreneurs must navigate ambiguity and adapt to changing circumstances.
3. *Competition*: Competition is fierce in most industries. Entrepreneurs must

differentiate their offerings and stay ahead of rivals.

4. *Resource Constraints*: Startups often have limited resources, including manpower. This necessitates efficient resource management.

5. *Work-Life Balance:* Entrepreneurship can be demanding, often requiring long hours and dedication. Achieving a work-life balance is a persistent challenge.

The Transformative Impact of Entrepreneurship

Entrepreneurship extends beyond individual financial success. It fosters economic growth, job creation, and innovation. Successful entrepreneurs become role models, inspiring others to pursue their dreams and contribute to society. Additionally, entrepreneurship promotes a culture of problem-solving and resilience, values that permeate various aspects of life.

Passive Income

Passive income is the golden ticket in the world of finance. It's the revenue stream that flows into your bank account without requiring constant effort or active participation. In this extensive exploration, we delve into the multifaceted realm of passive income, uncovering its importance, sources, strategies, and the transformative impact it can have on financial freedom.

Understanding Passive Income

1. *Importance*: Passive income is crucial for achieving financial security and independence. It allows individuals to supplement their active income, create wealth, and eventually attain financial freedom.
2. *Diverse Sources:* Passive income can be generated from a wide range of sources, including investments, rental properties, royalties, dividend-paying stocks, online businesses, and more.
3. *Wealth Preservation*: Passive income serves as a means to preserve and grow wealth over time. It's a buffer against financial setbacks and market volatility.

Sources of Passive Income

1. **Dividend Stocks**: Investing in dividend-paying stocks provides regular income through dividend payments. These stocks are often associated with stable, mature companies.
2. **Real Estate:** Rental properties, real estate investment trusts (REITs), and real estate crowdfunding platforms offer opportunities for passive income through property ownership.
3. **Peer-to-Peer Lending**: Online lending platforms enable individuals to lend money to borrowers and earn interest income.
4. **Royalties**: Creators, such as authors, musicians, and artists, can earn royalties from their intellectual property, including books, music, and art.

5. *Business Ownership*: Passive income can be generated from owning a business where you have minimal day-to-day involvement. This may involve hiring a manager or using automation.

6. *Digital Products and Online Businesses:* Creating and selling digital products like e-books, online courses, or software can generate passive income.

Strategies for Building Passive Income

1. *Investing for Income*: Tailor your investment portfolio to prioritize income-generating assets like dividend stocks and bonds.

2. *Real Estate Investment*: Invest in rental properties or consider REITs for exposure to real estate without direct property management.
3. *Business Ownership:* Start or acquire businesses that can be systematized and run with minimal hands-on involvement.
4. *Create Digital Products*: Develop digital products or content that can be sold repeatedly without ongoing effort.
5. *Royalties and Licensing:* If you possess intellectual property, explore licensing agreements or partnerships that generate ongoing royalties.
6. *Automatic Savings and Investments*: Set up automatic contributions to savings accounts or investment

accounts to accumulate passive income over time.

Challenges and Considerations

1. *Initial Effort*: Building passive income often requires significant upfront effort, whether in the form of investments, property management, or business setup.
2. *Risk Management*: Diversify your passive income sources to mitigate risk. Over-reliance on a single source can be precarious.
3. *Market Volatility*: Some passive income sources, such as stocks, can be subject to market fluctuations. A well-balanced portfolio can help manage this risk.

4. *Legal and Tax Considerations:* Depending on your passive income sources and location, tax implications and legal obligations may vary. Consult with experts to navigate these complexities.

The Transformative Impact of Passive Income

Passive income is a game-changer in the journey to financial independence. It offers freedom from the constraints of a traditional 9-to-5 job, providing individuals with the time and resources to pursue their passions, spend quality time with loved ones, and explore new opportunities. Passive income is the key to achieving the dream of financial freedom, allowing you to build wealth while you sleep and create a life on your terms.

Financial Assets: The Cornerstones of Wealth and Investment

Financial assets are the building blocks of modern finance and investment. They encompass a vast array of instruments and investments that hold monetary value and generate returns. In this extensive exploration, we delve into the multifaceted world of financial assets, understanding their types, functions, valuation, and the pivotal role they play in wealth creation and economic growth.

Types of Financial Assets

1. *Equity Securities*: These represent ownership in a company and include:
   - *Common Stocks*: Offer ownership in a company and the potential for capital appreciation and dividends.
   - *Preferred Stocks*: Provide fixed dividends and have preference over common stockholders in receiving dividends and assets in case of liquidation.
2. *Debt Securities*: These are forms of borrowing and include:
   - *Bonds*: Issued by governments or corporations, bonds pay periodic interest and return the principal upon maturity.
   - *Treasury Securities*: Issued by governments, these include

Treasury bills, notes, and bonds, known for their safety.

- ○ *Corporate Bonds*: Issued by corporations, they offer higher yields but carry credit risk.

3. **Derivatives**: Financial contracts deriving their value from an underlying asset. They include options, futures, and swaps, used for hedging or speculative purposes.

4. **Cash Equivalents:** Highly liquid investments with a short-term horizon, including Treasury bills, certificates of deposit (CDs), and money market funds.

5. **Real Estate Investment Trusts (REITs):** These allow investment in real estate properties, offering a share of rental income and property appreciation.

6. **Commodities**: Tangible assets like gold, oil, or agricultural products traded on commodities exchanges.
7. **Collectibles**: Items like art, antiques, or rare coins that can appreciate in value over time.

Functions and Significance

1. **Wealth Preservation**: Financial assets provide a means to preserve and grow wealth over time, serving as a store of value.
2. **Capital Allocation**: They facilitate the allocation of capital to businesses and governments, enabling economic growth.
3. **Income Generation:** Many financial assets, such as bonds or

dividend-paying stocks, provide regular income through interest or dividends.

4. *Risk Management:* Derivatives allow investors to manage risk, hedge against adverse price movements, and enhance portfolio diversification.

Valuation of Financial Assets

1. *Equity Valuation*: Common methods include price-to-earnings (P/E) ratios, discounted cash flows (DCF), and comparative market analysis.

2. *Bond Valuation:* Bonds are valued using present value calculations of their future cash flows, considering factors like coupon rate and time to maturity.

3. **Derivative Pricing:** Complex mathematical models, such as the Black-Scholes model for options, are used to determine derivative prices.

Risks Associated with Financial Assets

1. **Market Risk**: The potential for losses due to overall market fluctuations.
2. **Credit Risk:** The risk of issuer defaulting on interest or principal payments (applies to bonds and debt instruments).
3. **Liquidity Risk**: Difficulty in buying or selling assets without affecting their market price.
4. **Interest Rate Risk**: The impact of changes in interest rates on bond prices.

5. *Currency Risk*: Fluctuations in exchange rates that affect the value of foreign investments.

Diversification and Portfolio Management

Investors often diversify their portfolios by holding various types of financial assets. Diversification helps spread risk and can enhance returns. Portfolio management involves selecting assets, determining their allocation, and regularly reviewing and rebalancing the portfolio.

The Transformative Impact of Financial Assets

Financial assets are the catalysts of wealth creation and economic development. They allow individuals to invest in businesses, governments to fund infrastructure, and institutions to manage risk. By investing in financial assets wisely, individuals can build wealth over time, achieve financial goals, and secure their financial future.

Part III

Success in Action

Success is not merely the result of wishful thinking or a positive mindset; it's the outcome of deliberate actions and consistent efforts. In this extensive exploration, we dive deep into the realm of success in action, examining the critical components, practical strategies, and real-life stories that showcase how individuals transform their aspirations into concrete achievements.

The Components of Success

1. *Clear Goals*: Success begins with setting clear, specific goals. These

objectives provide direction and purpose, serving as the roadmap for your journey.

2. **Motivation**: Intrinsic motivation, driven by passion and a sense of purpose, propels individuals to take action even in the face of challenges.

3. **Planning**: A well-structured plan breaks down larger goals into manageable steps, making them less daunting and more achievable.

4. **Action**: Success requires action. Taking the first step and maintaining consistent effort are fundamental to progress.

5. **Resilience**: Setbacks and failures are inevitable. Resilience involves bouncing back from adversity, learning from mistakes, and persisting despite obstacles.

Strategies for Success in Action

1. **Time Management:** Effective time management ensures that you allocate your most valuable resource—time—toward meaningful tasks and goals. Techniques like the Pomodoro Technique and time blocking can enhance productivity.
2. **Resource Allocation:** Allocate resources wisely, whether it's finances, energy, or talent. Focus on high-impact activities that align with your goals.
3. **Continuous Learning**: Lifelong learning expands your knowledge and skills, enhancing your ability to adapt to changing circumstances and seize opportunities.

4. *Networking and Collaboration:* Building relationships and collaborating with others can open doors, provide support, and offer diverse perspectives.
5. *Mentorship*: Seek guidance from mentors who have achieved what you aspire to accomplish. Their experience and insights can accelerate your progress.

Case Studies in Success

1. *Entrepreneurial Triumph*: Explore stories of entrepreneurs who turned innovative ideas into successful businesses. Learn from their experiences of identifying

opportunities, overcoming challenges, and scaling their ventures.

2. *Investment Mastery:* Discover how savvy investors have navigated financial markets, managed risks, and achieved impressive returns on their investments. These case studies shed light on the strategies and principles behind successful investing.

3. *Leadership and Influence*: Leaders who've made a significant impact in their fields share their journeys. Their stories highlight the importance of vision, adaptability, and effective leadership in achieving success.

4. *Overcoming Adversity*: Many individuals have faced formidable obstacles on their path to success, from personal setbacks to societal barriers. These stories illustrate the

power of resilience, determination, and a growth mindset in surmounting challenges.

Sustainable Success and Giving Back

True success transcends personal achievement; it involves giving back to society. Successful individuals who've made significant contributions to their communities and causes share their philanthropic endeavors. Discover how success can be a catalyst for positive change and social impact.

The Role of Personal Growth

Success is not static; it's an ongoing journey of growth. Continuously challenging yourself, expanding your horizons, and embracing change are essential components of long-term success. Whether through personal development courses, reading, or seeking new experiences, personal growth ensures that you remain adaptable and receptive to new opportunities.

THREE

Learning from Real Stories

Human history is a tapestry woven with countless stories—narratives of triumph and adversity, of innovation and tradition, of dreams realized and challenges overcome. These stories are not just tales for entertainment; they are wellsprings of wisdom, fountains of knowledge, and invaluable sources of inspiration. In this extensive exploration, we dive deep into the realm of learning from real stories, understanding how the experiences of others can illuminate our own paths, and how narratives shape the way we perceive the world.

The Power of Real Stories

1. *Inspiration*: Real stories of achievement, resilience, and transformation inspire us to strive for our own aspirations. They demonstrate what is possible, igniting our imagination and motivation.
2. *Learning*: Stories are powerful teaching tools. They offer lessons in the form of lived experiences, imparting practical knowledge and insights that can be applied to various aspects of life.
3. *Perspective*: Real stories broaden our perspective, allowing us to see the world through the eyes of others. They foster empathy, understanding, and a deeper connection to the human experience.
4. *Resilience*: Tales of individuals who have overcome challenges remind us

of the strength of the human spirit. They serve as reminders that setbacks can be stepping stones to greater achievements.

Learning from Real Stories

1. *Biographies and Autobiographies:* Explore the life stories of historical figures, leaders, and innovators. Biographies and autobiographies provide in-depth insights into their journeys, strategies, and mindset.
2. *Case Studies:* Business and academic case studies analyze real-world situations, providing valuable lessons in decision-making, problem-solving, and strategy.

3. **Documentaries and Films**: Visual storytelling can be a compelling way to learn. Documentaries and films based on true stories bring history and contemporary issues to life, making them accessible and relatable.
4. **Oral Histories:** Personal interviews and oral histories capture the voices and experiences of individuals from diverse backgrounds, offering a rich tapestry of perspectives.

Lessons from Real Stories

1. **Resilience and Perseverance:** Stories of individuals who faced insurmountable odds and persevered against adversity teach us the importance of resilience,

determination, and unwavering belief in one's goals.

2. **Innovation and Creativity:** Innovators and inventors' stories inspire us to think outside the box, challenge conventions, and foster creativity in our endeavors.

3. **Leadership and Influence**: Leadership narratives highlight the qualities of effective leaders—vision, empathy, and the ability to inspire and guide others.

4. **Ethics and Values:** Real stories often showcase moral dilemmas and ethical choices. They prompt reflection on our own values and principles.

Applying Real Stories to Your Life

1. *Identify Role Models:* Identify individuals whose stories resonate with your aspirations. Study their journeys and draw inspiration from their experiences.

2. *Extract Practical Insights*: Analyze real stories for practical insights and actionable takeaways. Consider how the lessons learned can be applied to your own life and goals.

3. *Share and Discuss*: Engage in discussions with others about the stories you've encountered. Sharing insights and perspectives can deepen your understanding and offer new insights.

4. *Document Your Own Journey*: Your life is a story in the making. Document your experiences, challenges, and

triumphs. Your narrative may inspire others on their own journeys.

The Impact of Real Stories on Society

Real stories not only shape individuals but also influence society. They can drive social change, challenge stereotypes, and foster empathy among diverse communities. When shared and celebrated, real stories become a powerful force for understanding, unity, and progress.

A few of these stories we've seen are;

1. **Steve Jobs - Innovation and Resilience:** Steve Jobs co-founded Apple Inc. and revolutionized the tech industry. He was fired from Apple at one point but returned to lead the

company to even greater heights. His story teaches us about the importance of innovation, resilience, and the pursuit of a vision.

2. *Nelson Mandela - Perseverance and Leadership:* Nelson Mandela spent 27 years in prison for his role in the anti-apartheid struggle in South Africa. Upon his release, he became the country's first black president and worked towards reconciliation and justice. His story showcases the power of perseverance, leadership, and forgiveness.

3. *Malala Yousafzai - Advocacy and Courage:* Malala Yousafzai, a Pakistani activist for girls' education, survived an assassination attempt by the Taliban and went on to become a global advocate for education and

women's rights. Her story highlights the importance of standing up for what you believe in, even in the face of danger.

4. *Warren Buffett - Investment Mastery*: Warren Buffett, one of the world's most successful investors, started with a small investment and built a vast fortune. His story teaches us about the principles of long-term investing, value assessment, and patience in wealth-building.

5. *Elon Musk - Vision and Entrepreneurship:* Elon Musk co-founded PayPal, Tesla, SpaceX, and other groundbreaking companies. His story illustrates the power of visionary thinking, entrepreneurship, and the willingness to take bold risks to achieve ambitious goals.

6. *Harriet Tubman - Courage and Freedom:* Harriet Tubman escaped slavery and then risked her life to help other enslaved people reach freedom through the Underground Railroad. Her story is a testament to courage, determination, and the fight for justice.

7. *Anne Frank - Resilience and Hope:* Anne Frank's diary, written during her time in hiding from the Nazis during World War II, is a poignant account of resilience, hope, and the enduring power of the human spirit in the face of adversity.

8. *Oprah Winfrey - Overcoming Adversity*: Oprah Winfrey overcame a difficult childhood and built a media empire. Her story is one of resilience, determination, and the ability to

transform personal challenges into opportunities for growth and success.

Resilience and Networking

Resilience and networking are two indispensable pillars that support the structure of personal and professional success. Resilience is the ability to bounce back from adversity, while networking involves building valuable relationships and connections. In this extensive exploration, we delve into the symbiotic relationship between resilience and networking, understanding their significance, strategies for cultivation, and how they jointly propel individuals toward their goals.

Resilience: The Foundation of Success

1. *The Importance of Resilience*:
   Resilience is the mental and
   emotional strength that enables
   individuals to withstand challenges,
   adapt to change, and emerge stronger
   from setbacks. It's a key determinant
   of long-term success.
2. *Components of Resilience*:
   - *Emotional Regulation:* Resilient
     individuals can manage their
     emotions effectively, avoiding
     being overwhelmed by stress or
     setbacks.
   - *Adaptability*: Being open to
     change and adaptable is crucial
     for resilience. It allows
     individuals to respond to new
     circumstances and challenges
     with flexibility.

- *Optimism*: Maintaining a positive outlook, even in the face of difficulties, is a hallmark of resilience. Optimism fosters the belief that challenges can be overcome.

3. **Cultivating Resilience:**
   - *Mindfulness and Self-Care*: Practices like mindfulness meditation and self-care routines can enhance emotional resilience.
   - *Learning from Setbacks:* Viewing failures and setbacks as opportunities for growth and learning is a key aspect of resilience.
   - *Seeking Support:* Building a support network of friends, family, or mentors can provide

valuable emotional support
during challenging times.

Networking: The Bridge to Opportunities

1. *The Power of Networking*:
   Networking involves building and
   maintaining relationships with others,
   both personally and professionally. It
   opens doors to opportunities,
   information, and resources that can
   propel one's career or personal
   pursuits.
2. *Types of Networks:*
   ○ *Personal Networks:* These
     include friends, family, and
     acquaintances. Personal
     networks provide emotional
     support and social connections.

- *Professional Networks:* Professional networks consist of colleagues, mentors, industry peers, and business contacts. They offer career-related opportunities and insights.

3. **Strategies for Effective Networking:**
   - *Authenticity*: Authenticity and genuine interest in others are the cornerstones of effective networking. People respond positively to authenticity.
   - *Reciprocity*: Networking is a two-way street. Offering help or support to others fosters goodwill and strengthens relationships.
   - *Visibility*: Actively participating in industry events, conferences, and online forums can enhance

visibility and expand your professional network.

- *Follow-Up*: Consistent follow-up is essential. Stay in touch with contacts, share updates, and nurture relationships over time.

The Synergy Between Resilience and Networking

1. *Resilience Enhances Networking:*
    - Resilient individuals can handle rejection or setbacks in networking efforts without becoming discouraged.
    - They are more likely to persist in building relationships, even

when faced with initial challenges.

2. **Networking Supports Resilience:**
   - A robust professional network can provide emotional support during difficult times.
   - Networking connections may offer insights, advice, or opportunities that can aid in overcoming obstacles.

3. **Case Studies in Resilience and Networking:**
   - *J.K. Rowling:* The author of the Harry Potter series faced numerous rejections before achieving success. Her resilience and later networking within the literary world propelled her to fame.

- *Elon Musk:* Musk faced significant setbacks with his early startups but leveraged his network to secure funding and partnerships, ultimately achieving success with companies like SpaceX and Tesla.

Building a Resilience-Networking Loop

1. **Set Goals**: Define your goals, both in terms of resilience and networking. What challenges do you want to overcome, and what connections do you aim to build?
2. **Cultivate Resilience:** Work on developing emotional regulation,

adaptability, and optimism. Seek support and learn from setbacks.

3. *Network Authentically*: Build relationships genuinely, based on shared interests and mutual benefit. Be open to giving and receiving support.

4. *Leverage Networking for Resilience:* Use your network for emotional support, guidance, and opportunities that enhance your resilience.

5. *Apply Resilience to Networking:* When faced with setbacks in networking, draw upon your resilience to persist and learn from experiences.

Philanthropy

Philanthropy is the noble endeavour of using one's resources, whether financial, time, or expertise, to promote the well-being of others and to address pressing social issues. It's a powerful force for positive change, contributing to the betterment of communities, society at large, and even the world. In this extensive exploration, we delve deep into the realm of philanthropy, understanding its significance, the motivations behind it, the various forms it can take, and its transformative impact on individuals and society.

The Significance of Philanthropy

1. *Addressing Inequities:* Philanthropy plays a pivotal role in addressing social, economic, and environmental inequalities. It provides resources to

those who need them the most, helping to level the playing field.

2. *Social Innovation:* Philanthropy supports innovation and experimentation in finding solutions to complex problems. It funds research, pilot projects, and initiatives that can lead to transformative change.

3. *Community Building:* Philanthropy fosters a sense of community and connectedness. It encourages individuals and organizations to collaborate, share resources, and work towards common goals.

4. *Catalyst for Change*: Philanthropic initiatives often serve as catalysts for broader systemic change. They can influence policies, inspire others to

give, and create ripple effects of positive impact.

Motivations for Philanthropy

1. **Personal Values**: Many philanthropists are driven by their personal values and a deep sense of social responsibility. They believe in using their resources for the greater good.
2. **Desire for Impact:** Philanthropists often have a genuine desire to make a meaningful impact on pressing issues, whether it's education, healthcare, poverty alleviation, or environmental conservation.
3. **Legacy and Meaning:** Some individuals see philanthropy as a way

to leave a lasting legacy and find meaning in their wealth or life's work.

4. *Gratitude and Empathy*: Experiences of gratitude or empathy for others' suffering can motivate philanthropy. Witnessing the struggles of others can inspire a desire to help.

Forms of Philanthropy

1. *Financial Contributions*: This is the most common form of philanthropy, involving donations to charitable organizations, foundations, or causes.
2. *Volunteerism*: Giving one's time and expertise through volunteer work is a valuable form of philanthropy. It can involve mentoring, teaching, or direct involvement in community projects.

3. *Impact Investing:* Some philanthropists choose to invest their funds in projects or businesses that have both a financial return and a positive social or environmental impact.

4. *Corporate Philanthropy:* Companies often engage in philanthropic efforts through corporate social responsibility (CSR) initiatives, donating a portion of their profits or resources to charitable causes.

5. *Foundations*: Establishing foundations or trusts dedicated to specific causes is another form of philanthropy. These organisations can have a lasting impact by directing resources over time.

The Transformative Impact of Philanthropy

1. *Alleviating Human Suffering:* Philanthropy provides relief to those in need, offering food, shelter, healthcare, and education to vulnerable populations.
2. *Supporting Education:* Many educational institutions and scholarships are funded through philanthropy, opening doors to learning and personal development.
3. *Advancing Scientific Research:* Philanthropy has contributed to groundbreaking scientific research, leading to medical discoveries, technological advancements, and innovations that benefit humanity.

4. *Environmental Conservation:*
   Philanthropic efforts support
   environmental causes, aiding in the
   preservation of natural ecosystems
   and the fight against climate change.

5. *Empowering Communities:*
   Philanthropy empowers communities
   to take control of their destinies,
   fostering self-reliance and sustainable
   development.

6. *Promoting Social Justice:*
   Philanthropic initiatives often aim to
   address systemic injustices, promote
   equality, and advance civil rights.

Challenges in Philanthropy

1. *Effective Giving:* Ensuring that
   philanthropic resources are used

effectively and efficiently to achieve intended outcomes can be challenging.

2. *Sustainability*: Maintaining long-term impact and continuity of philanthropic efforts can be difficult, especially when addressing complex, deeply rooted issues.

3. *Ethical Considerations:* Ethical questions may arise in philanthropy, such as determining the best ways to support causes without inadvertently causing harm.

4. *Measuring Impact:* Quantifying the impact of philanthropic initiatives and determining success metrics can be complex.

The Future of Philanthropy

Philanthropy continues to evolve with innovations like impact investing, social enterprises, and strategic partnerships. In an interconnected world, philanthropy transcends borders, with global challenges demanding collaborative solutions.

Part IV

Challenges and Beyond

Success, while a worthy pursuit, is not a straightforward path paved with unbroken triumphs. It's a journey filled with challenges, obstacles, and complexities that require resilience, adaptability, and ethical considerations. In this extensive exploration, we delve into the multifaceted nature of challenges on the road to success and how individuals can transcend them to achieve not only their financial goals but also personal fulfillment and positive impact on society.

FOUR

Handling Setbacks

In the quest for success, setbacks are not detours but essential waypoints. They are the storms that test the resilience of the traveler on the road to their goals. Understanding how to handle setbacks is a critical skill that separates those who persevere from those who falter. This exploration delves into the nature of setbacks, strategies for managing them, and the profound lessons they offer on the road to success.

The Nature of Setbacks

Setbacks are the unexpected hurdles, failures, or obstacles that disrupt the smooth progress toward a goal. They come in various forms: financial losses, project failures, personal challenges, or unforeseen external factors. While they can be disheartening, setbacks are an inevitable part of any ambitious journey.

Strategies for Managing Setbacks

1. *Resilience*: Resilience is the ability to bounce back from adversity. It involves maintaining a positive attitude, seeking solutions, and learning from setbacks. Resilient individuals view setbacks as opportunities for growth.
2. *Adaptability*: Success often requires the ability to adapt to changing circumstances. Setbacks can signal the need for a change in strategy or

approach. Flexibility and the willingness to pivot are crucial.

3. **Problem-Solving**: Setbacks are challenges that demand creative problem-solving. They invite individuals to analyze the situation, identify root causes, and develop effective solutions.

4. **Learning and Growth**: Setbacks provide valuable lessons. They highlight weaknesses, offer insights, and allow for personal and professional growth. Embracing setbacks as learning opportunities can be transformative.

5. **Support Systems:** Seek support from mentors, peers, or a trusted network during setbacks. They can offer guidance, encouragement, and perspective.

The Profound Lessons of Setbacks

1. *Resilience and Grit:* Setbacks test one's resolve and resilience. They reveal the depth of determination and grit required to overcome challenges.
2. *Adaptation and Innovation:* Setbacks foster adaptability and innovation. They push individuals to find new approaches and creative solutions to problems.
3. *Character Building:* How one handles setbacks speaks volumes about their character. Perseverance, integrity, and humility shine through adversity.
4. *Refinement of Goals:* Setbacks often lead to a reevaluation of goals. They help individuals clarify their objectives and refine their strategies.

5. *Success with Wisdom*: Those who have weathered setbacks emerge wiser and more prepared for future challenges. Success, when achieved after overcoming setbacks, is tempered with wisdom.

Continuous Learning

In the ever-evolving landscape of today's world, the concept of continuous learning has transcended the boundaries of formal education to become a dynamic necessity for personal and professional growth. It embodies the idea that learning is not confined to a classroom or a specific stage of life but is a perpetual journey of exploration and self-improvement.

Continuous learning is a mindset that encourages individuals to seek new knowledge, develop new skills, and adapt to changing circumstances. It empowers them to stay relevant in their careers, embrace innovation, and thrive in an increasingly competitive global environment.

Moreover, continuous learning fuels creativity, fosters adaptability, and enhances problem-solving abilities. It opens doors to new opportunities and perspectives, broadening horizons and enriching lives. Whether through reading, online courses, mentorship, or experiential learning, the commitment to continuous learning is an investment in one's future and a testament to the resilience of the human spirit.

Work-Life Balance

In our fast-paced, modern world, achieving a harmonious work-life balance is a pursuit that lies at the heart of individual well-being and overall life satisfaction. This equilibrium between professional commitments and personal life is not merely an aspiration but a fundamental necessity for a fulfilling and sustainable life journey.

Work-life balance is a state where individuals can effectively juggle their work responsibilities, career ambitions, and personal lives, including family, relationships, hobbies, and self-care. Here's why it's so crucial:

1. *Health and Well-being*: Maintaining a balance between work and personal life is paramount for physical and mental health. Neglecting one in favor of the other can lead to stress, burnout, and various health issues.

2. *Enhanced Productivity:* Paradoxically, dedicating excessive hours to work can diminish productivity. A well-rested and rejuvenated mind is more creative, focused, and efficient.

3. *Nurturing Relationships:* Personal relationships are the bedrock of a fulfilling life. Striking a balance allows individuals to invest time and energy into meaningful connections with family and friends.

4. *Self-Care:* Prioritising self-care is a vital component of work-life balance. It involves

activities that rejuvenate the mind and body, such as exercise, meditation, hobbies, and leisure.

5. *Personal Fulfillment:* Success in the workplace is meaningful when it aligns with personal fulfillment. A balanced life allows individuals to pursue their passions, interests, and personal growth.

Achieving work-life balance requires deliberate effort and planning:

1. *Set Boundaries:* Establish clear boundaries between work and personal life. Define specific work hours and adhere to them to prevent work from encroaching on personal time.

2. *Prioritise and Delegate:* Identify your most important tasks and prioritize them.

Delegate tasks when possible, both at work and home, to lighten your load.

3. *Learn to Say No:* Don't overcommit yourself. Politely decline additional work or personal obligations when you feel overwhelmed.

4. *Schedule Personal Time:* Just as you schedule work-related meetings and tasks, schedule personal time for relaxation, family, and activities you enjoy.

5. *Unplug*: Disconnect from work emails and notifications during your personal time to truly unwind and be present with loved ones.

6. *Seek Support*: Lean on your support network, whether it's family, friends, or colleagues. Communicate your needs and

challenges to receive assistance and understanding.

Legacy Planning

Legacy planning is the deliberate and thoughtful process of crafting the mark you'll leave on the world. It's not limited to wealth distribution but encompasses the values, knowledge, and contributions you'll be remembered for. Legacy planning involves creating a roadmap to ensure your assets benefit future generations or causes close to your heart. It may include wills, trusts, charitable contributions, and imparting wisdom.

CONCLUSION

As we draw the final curtain on this journey, "the road to $100 Million: Mastering the Nine-Figure Mindset," it's essential to reflect on the profound lessons and transformative insights shared along the way. This book has been a roadmap, guiding you through the intricate terrain of financial mastery, personal growth, and societal impact. It's a reminder that success, whether defined by wealth, fulfillment, or legacy, is not an isolated destination but an ever-evolving journey.

Throughout our exploration, we've delved into the core principles of mindset, resilience, ethical decision-making, work-life balance, and continuous learning. We've uncovered the significance of philanthropy, legacy, and giving back. We've navigated the complexities of success, including the inevitable setbacks that challenge us to grow. We've emphasized that success is not merely about personal achievements but about the positive impact we leave on the world.

The Ongoing Journey

Success is not a static destination but an ever-evolving journey. This concluding chapter emphasizes that the pursuit of success is continuous and dynamic. It underscores the importance of lifelong learning, adaptability, and personal growth. By embracing change and staying grounded in one's values, individuals can navigate the complexities of success with resilience and authenticity.

Navigating the Complexities of Success

1. *Resilience in Adversity:* Learn from individuals who have faced adversity and emerged stronger. Discover how setbacks can be catalysts for growth and how resilience is key to overcoming challenges.
2. *Ethical Decision-Making:* Grapple with ethical dilemmas and explore the principles that guide ethical choices. Understand the importance of upholding personal and societal values on the road to success.
3. *Balancing Success and Well-being*: Prioritize well-being as an integral

part of success. Find strategies to maintain physical and mental health while pursuing ambitious goals.

4. *Legacy and Giving Back:* Recognize the potential for positive impact beyond personal success. Explore avenues for contributing to society and leaving a meaningful legacy.

5. *The Unending Quest for Growth:* Embrace the idea that success is a lifelong journey. Understand that personal growth, adaptability, and continuous learning are essential components of enduring success.

APPENDIX

In this appendix, you'll find a curated list of resources to further your exploration of the principles and concepts discussed in "the road to $100 Million: Mastering the Nine-Figure Mindset." These resources encompass books, websites, organizations, and tools that can enhance your understanding and support your ongoing journey towards financial mastery and personal fulfillment.

Books

1. *Mindset: The New Psychology of Success by Carol S. Dweck* - Dive deeper into the concept of mindset

and how it can shape your path to success.

2. *Grit: The Power of Passion and Perseverance by Angela Duckworth* - Explore the role of grit and determination in achieving your long-term goals.

3. *The Lean Startup: How Today's Entrepreneurs Use Continuous Innovation to Create Radically Successful Businesses by Eric Ries* - Learn about innovative approaches to entrepreneurship and business growth.

4. *Give and Take: Why Helping Others Drives Our Success by Adam Grant* - Delve into the idea of giving back and its impact on personal and professional success.

Websites and Online Courses

1. *Coursera (coursera.org)* - Offers a wide range of online courses on entrepreneurship, leadership, and personal development.
2. *TED Talks (ted.com)* - Features inspiring talks on various topics related to success, mindset, and personal growth.
3. *MindTools (mindtools.com)* - Provides practical tools and resources for personal and career development.
4. *Khan Academy (khanacademy.org)* - Offers free educational resources on a variety of subjects, including finance and economics.

Organisations and Communities

1. *Young Presidents' Organization (YPO)* - A global network of young chief executives dedicated to lifelong learning and idea exchange.
2. *Toastmasters International (toastmasters.org)* - Join a local Toastmasters club to improve your public speaking and leadership skills.
3. *SCORE (score.org)* - A nonprofit organization that offers free mentoring to small business owners and entrepreneurs.

Tools for Financial Planning

1. *Mint (mint.com)* - A free budgeting tool that helps you track your expenses, set financial goals, and manage your finances effectively.

2. *Personal Capital (personalcapital.com)* - Offers tools for tracking and managing your investments, retirement planning, and financial goals.
3. *Trello (trello.com)* - A project management tool that can help you organize and plan your personal and professional goals.

Philanthropic Resources

1. *Charitable Giving Guide (givingcompass.org)* - Provides resources and insights on effective philanthropy and charitable giving.
2. *GuideStar (guidestar.org)* - Offers information on nonprofit organizations and their impact,

helping you make informed
philanthropic decisions.

Legacy Planning and Estate Resources

1. *AARP Estate Planning Guide
   (aarp.org)* - Provides comprehensive
   information on estate planning, wills,
   trusts, and legacy considerations.
2. *National Association of Estate
   Planners & Councils (naepc.org)* -
   Offers resources and information on
   estate planning professionals and
   practices.

Additional Reading

1. *Forbes (forbes.com)* - Explore Forbes
   articles and interviews with

successful individuals for insights and inspiration.
2. *Harvard Business Review (hbr.org)* - Access articles and research on leadership, management, and personal development.

www.ingramcontent.com/pod-product-compliance
Lightning Source LLC
Chambersburg PA
CBHW062328290526
45794CB00005B/1944